Commissioned by the Cardiff Polyphonic Choir

AVE REX
A Carol Sequence

Anonymous Mediaeval words

WILLIAM MATHIAS
(Opus 45)

I AVE REX

Duration: c. 14 minutes

This work was first performed, with organ accompaniment, at Llandaff Cathedral on 6th December 1969 by the Cardiff Polyphonic Choir with Richard Elfyn Jones (organ) conducted by Roy Bohana.
It is scored for double w.w., 4 hn., 3 tpt., 3 tmb., tuba, timp., perc. (2 players), organ (or piano), and strings.
Full scores, vocal scores, and orchestral parts are on hire.

2

TENORS and BASSES UNIS. *f*

Hail,__ most migh-ty in thy work-ing,__

A

Gt. (*f*)

Tpt.

Ped.   16' only

Hail,__ thou Lord of all thing,__

Tpt.

I   of - fer__ thee   Gold__

ff

ff

8' + 16'

Ave Rex

4

✛ See page 31

Ave Rex

Ave Rex

-ve, A - ve prin - ceps - que, prin - ceps - que pol - o - rum.

A - ve prin - ceps - que, prin - ceps - que pol - o - rum.

Hail,— most migh-ty in thy work-ing,

Hail,— most migh-ty in thy work-ing,

16' only Ped.

8' + 16'

Ave Rex

II ALLELUYA, A NEW WORK IS COME ON HAND

Ave Rex

12

Ave Rex

14

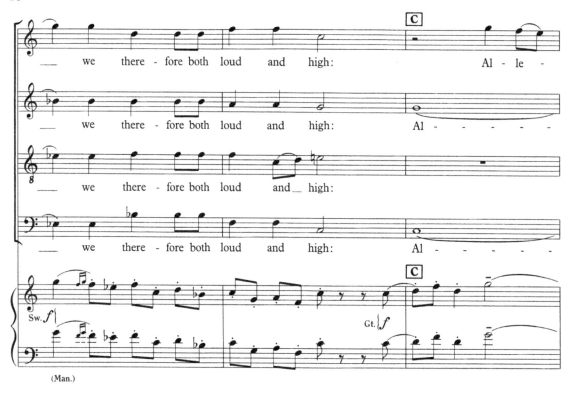

we there - fore both loud and high: Al - le -

we there - fore both loud and high: Al - - - -

we there - fore both loud and __ high:

we there - fore both loud and high: Al - - - -

Sw. *f* Gt. *f*

(Man.)

- lu - ya, al - le - lu - ya, al - le - lu - ya, al - le -

- - - - - - le - - - - - lu - - - -

Al - le - lu - ya, __ al - le - lu - ya, __ al - le - lu - ya,

- - - - - - - le - - - - - lu - - - - -

Ped.

Ave Rex

Ave Rex

III THERE IS NO ROSE OF SUCH VIRTUE

Tempo I, Lento flessibile (♩ = c. 76)

SOPRANOS

There is no rose___ of such vir-tue As is the rose___ that bare Je-su:

ORGAN

Man.

Tempo II, Allegretto (♩. = c. 72)

ALTO

Al-le-lu-ia,___ al-le-lu - - - - ia, al-le-lu-ia, al-le-

TENOR

Al - le - lu - ia, al - le-lu - ia,___ al - le - lu-

BASS

Al - le - lu - ia, al - le - lu - ia,___ al -

Tempo II, Allegretto (♩. = c. 72)

(Man.)

poco rit.

-lu - ia,___ al-le-lu - - - - - ia.

- - - - ia, al - le - lu - ia.___

- le - lu - ia.

poco rit.

18

Ave Rex

(Man.)

Ave Rex

Ave Rex

IV SIR CHRISTÈMAS

This number is published separately (X207) finishing at the end of the first line of page 31.

Ave Rex

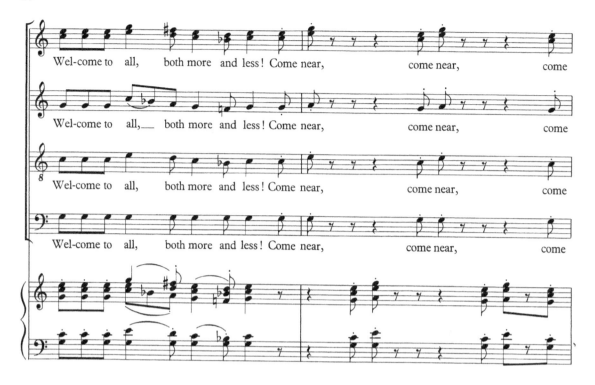

28

Ave Rex

tou - te la com - pag - nie.___(e)   Make good cheer and be right mer - ry, And

tou - te la com - pag - nie.___(e)   Make good cheer and be right mer - ry, And

sing with us now joy - ful - ly,___   joy - ful - ly,___   joy - ful - ly:___

sing with us now joy - ful - ly,___   joy - ful - ly,___   joy - ful - ly:___

Now - ell, now - ell,   now - ell, now - ell,   now - ell, now - ell, now - ell, now - ell,   now -

Now - ell, now - ell,   now - ell, now - ell,   now - ell, now - ell, now - ell, now - ell,   now -

(Attacca at ✛ on page 4)

Processed and printed by
Halstan & Co. Ltd., Amersham, Bucks., England

OXFORD UNIVERSITY PRESS